California's Central Coast

Including
Southern Monterey County
San Luis Obispo County
Santa Barbara County
Ventura County

DIVING AND SNORKELING GUIDE TO

California's Central Coast

Including
Southern Monterey County
San Luis Obispo County
Santa Barbara County
Ventura County

Darren Douglass

Pisces Books™
A division of Gulf Publishing Company
Houston, Texas

ACKNOWLEDGMENTS

He alone stretches out the heavens
and treads on the waves of the sea

Job 9:8

Pisces Books
A division of Gulf Publishing Company
P.O. Box 2608, Houston, Texas 77252-2608

Library of Congress Cataloging-in-Publication Data

Douglass, Darren.
Diving and snorkeling guide to California's central coast : including southern Monterey County, San Luis Obispo County, Santa Barbara County, Venture County / Darren Douglass.
p. cm.
Includes index.
ISBN 1-55992-079-3
1. Skin diving—California—Guidebooks. 2. Scuba diving—California—Guidebooks. 3. California—Guidebooks. I. Title. II. Title: Central California.
GV840.S78D65 1995
797.2′3—dc20 94-20893
CIP

Pisces Books is a trademark of Gulf Publishing Company.

Printed in Hong Kong

10 9 8 7 6 5 4 3 2 1

Publisher's note: At the time of publication of this book, all the information was determined to be as accurate as possible. However, when you use this guide, new construction may have changed land reference points, weather may have altered reef configurations, and some businesses may no longer be in operation. Your assistance in keeping future editions up-to-date will be greatly appreciated.

Also, please pay particular attention to the diver rating system in this book. Know your limits!

Table of Contents

Pfieffer Burns State Park, home of Partington Cove, provides some of the best, least crowded beaches in Big Sur.

How To Use This Guide

This guide is part of a two-volume set to acquaint you with California's best beach diving sites from the Big Sur coast to the Ventura/Los Angeles county line. Distant coastal reefs and island destinations are not included in this publications, just some of the best dive sites available off California beaches.

California has nearly 1,000 miles of coastline. The area between Big Sur in south Monterey county and Ventura county accounts for a large part of that area. There are numerous dive sites not mentioned here as it would take several texts to contain them. The Central California coast is uncrowded. Many rarely visited dive sites are here. This guide will focus on the best of the best. Central California is noted for its unspoiled and uncrowded beaches, but not all are suitable for diving. Each beach included in this guide was chosen because of its consistently good visibility, a variety of underwater flora and fauna, interesting terrain, proximity to shore, and reasonable access for divers. Some sites are reached best by boat. You may find yourself driving a distance to reach some of these locations too, but weather permitting, the diving is worthwhile. The coastline here is beautiful, and driving can actually become a pleasant experience. There are enough dive sites here to keep the most ardent diver busy for many weekends to come. Some dive sites here are more difficult to access and involve hiking down long trails with heavy gear.

Surf's up! Water conditions can become hazardous for beach dives along the Central California coast. It's important to carefully evaluate surf conditions before entering the water.

A playful California sea lion cavorts on the surface. Sea lions often frolic with beach divers along the Big Sur coast.

Some diving areas here are subject to oceanic and atmospheric conditions. All sites are affected by stormy weather from time to time. If you plan your diving day carefully, however, you'll enjoy what you find beneath the waves. Good luck and good diving.

Central coast diving can be arduous. Long hikes, strong current, surge, and strong winds affect diving conditions. It is important to evaluate dive site conditions and know your limitations. All dive areas listed in this guide require a degree of skill, but use common sense and good judgment if conditions preclude diving at your targeted site. Most areas here involve rocky entries and incoming surf. Be wise in the estimation of your abilities as you plan your underwater adventures off Central California's beaches.

Rating System for Divers and Dive Sites

A rating system (novice, intermediate, advanced) will be used throughout this guide. The reader should be aware that varying environmental conditions can make a novice dive site advanced and vice versa. Most diving between Ventura and Monterey involves intermediate skills at a minimum. Considerable beach and surf entry experience is required before attempting to dive off the beaches in this part of the Golden State. If you are visiting Central California and have not had this experience, you would be wise to venture seaward on the calmest of days only. Completing an environmental orientation with an instructor or divemaster is highly recommended as well. And you should, of course, be in good physical condition.

A *novice* diver is defined as a recently certified diver without a lot of experience. This rating also applies to a diver from another location making his or her first Central California beach dive or a diver who has been inactive.

An *intermediate* diver is one who has been certified for at least one year and has logged approximately 12 to 24 dives. An *advanced* diver does not have to have completed an advanced diving course, although one would certainly be beneficial. However, an *advanced* diver should have commensu-

A diver explores a picturesque kelp bed. Kelp divers will love California's central coast.

rate experience in many environments, including rocky beach diving with surf entries. A diver may only hold an entry level certification, but should have 50 or more logged dives and should be extremely comfortable in all types of water conditions.

Decide for yourself in which category you fall. Good divers will weigh experience, evaluate water conditions, and make a proper assessment to dive or not. Venturing inside caverns or caves is only suitable for those who have been trained and certified in this skilled field. Although unusual on a beach dive, some areas with nearby submarine canyons can put divers in 100 feet of water. The most important consideration for diving in this part of California coast environmental conditions. Diving the Central California coast is not for the untrained or ill-prepared. For the skillful, seasoned diver, however, special rewards that are unique to this area await.

1

Overview of Central California: Southern Monterey County to Ventura County

Climate. Central California is noted for its temperate weather with fog and drizzle. Inland temperatures are warm throughout most of the year but along the coast, temperatures can become downright cold. If you'll be staying along the coast, bring along a warm jacket. From December to March, coastal temperatures range from 40–60 °F. You should also carry an umbrella, as this is the rainy season in California. Temperatures rise slightly from April to early July, but expect fog and clouds during the morning and evening. Warm days are not uncommon, however. Although you can dive Central California year round, the best time to dive is late fall and early winter. There are fewer storms and water visibility is generally good.

Water Temperatures. Water temperatures follow the same cycle as air temperatures: 40–60 °F in the winter and 50–60° in the summer. Deeper waters are obviously colder. With these water temperatures, a good, warm, wetsuit is necessary. Some divers get by with a 6.5 mm dive suit, but a full 7 mm or ⅜ in. wetsuit and hood are often used with good success. Many central coast divers prefer to use a dry suit.

Beach Diving. Beach diving has several advantages over boat diving: it's inexpensive and offers personal mobility. There are just a few guidelines to follow in preparing for a beach dive, and some diving techniques to keep in mind. Beach diving does require some physical strength. You should have enough stamina to get in and out of the water, reach your offshore destination, and be able to handle an emergency. The best way to get in shape for beach diving is through some kind of aerobic exercise—running, cycling, dance, and swimming. Skin diving is an excellent conditioner for SCUBA.

Try to schedule your dives for the morning. The winds tend to be calmer this time of day. Crowds are rarely a problem. Also try to plan your dives during periods of high or incoming tides. The incoming tides bring in the clear offshore waters, creating better visibility. The higher water may also help you get by a shallow reef or rock on your swim out to the dive site. How-

Central California is well known for its cool climate and uncrowded coastline.▶

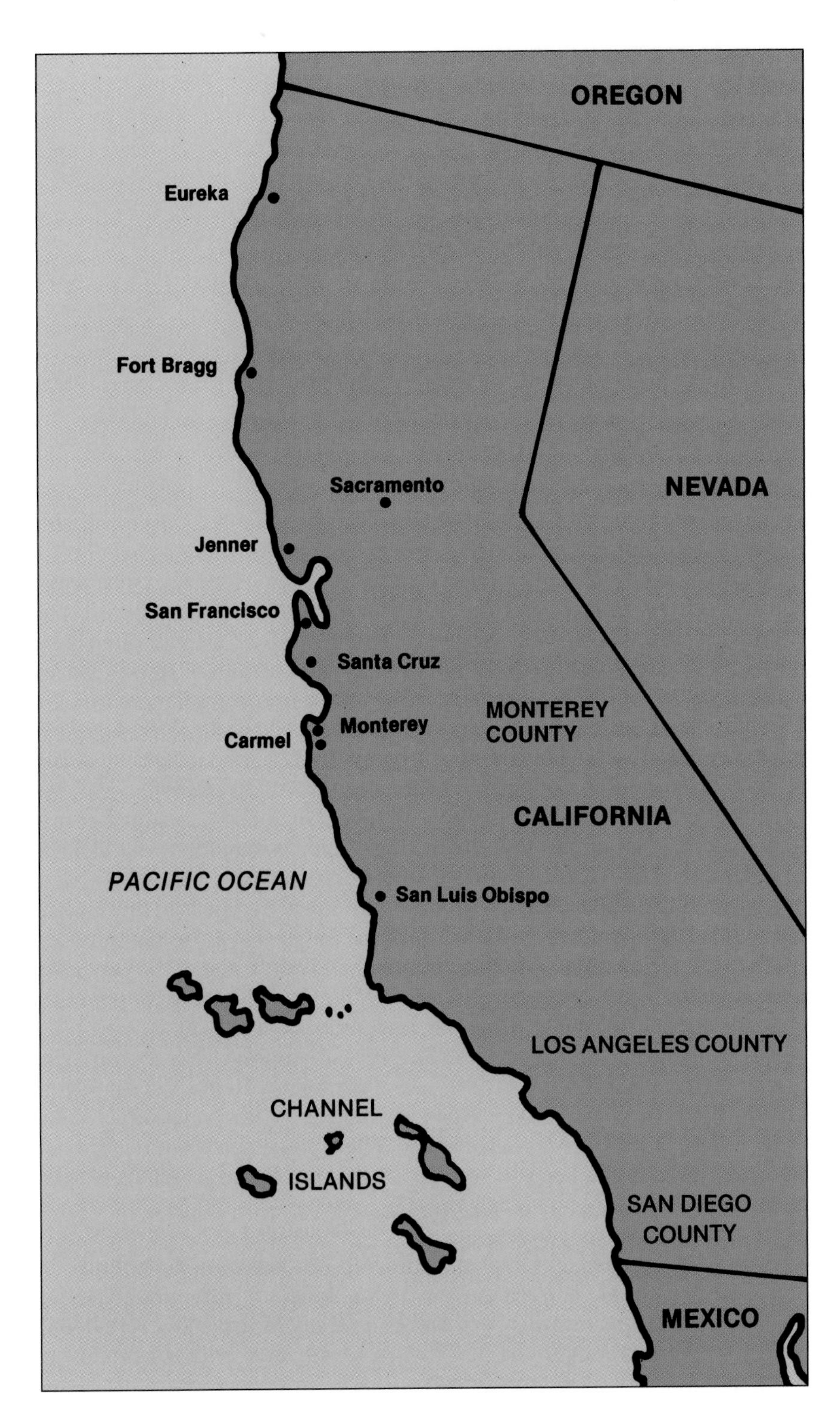
OREGON
Eureka
Fort Bragg
Sacramento
NEVADA
Jenner
San Francisco
Santa Cruz
Monterey
Carmel
MONTEREY
COUNTY
CALIFORNIA
PACIFIC OCEAN
San Luis Obispo
LOS ANGELES COUNTY
CHANNEL
ISLANDS
SAN DIEGO
COUNTY
MEXICO

Hiding inside his home in the reef, this little blenny poses nervously for a macro photographer's extension tube.

ever, there are some limitations when diving during high tide. Some beaches may become impassable and the surf may be more difficult to handle.

Always take time to fully evaluate conditions before suiting up. Upon arrival at the beach, take time to carefully observe conditions. Use binoculars to scout out hidden reefs or kelp beds. Watch the surf carefully. Surf will often come in "sets" of two to five big waves, followed by short periods of smaller waves. Time these sets. Look for rip tides, which can move you offshore quickly. Carefully check entry and exit points and always have an alternative entry/exit point in mind. Observe how the kelp is lying; this is a good indication of currents. If the current is ripping, look for a dive site that's calmer.

Move quickly when entering the surf zone. Do not stop to adjust gear or look back. Swim out past the surf then rest. This will reduce your chances of getting knocked down. Should you fall, stay down. If the water is deep enough (2–3 feet), kick out the rest of the way. Many experienced divers wade out to this depth and turn to swim. Take the larger waves by going underneath them. If you time your entry properly and don't stop in the surf zone, you probably won't have any problems. Waves may look bigger than they actually are; so relaxing and ducking under the surf is essential.

To exit the water, simply reverse the process. Approach the seaward side of the surf zone as closely as possible and wait there. Relax and catch your breath. Again, time the waves. Head for shore between wave sets.

Don't stop until you are high and dry. When you reach waist-deep water, stand up and back out, keeping your eye on the surf. If you get knocked down and can't get up, stay down and crawl in.

Kelp. Giant kelp beds, some extending up 100 feet from the bottom, are abundant in Central California. Kelp grows thick and very quickly, creating dense submarine forests which harbor a variety of fish and invertebrates. Kelp is only hazardous if you don't know how to deal with it. Perhaps the most important thing to remember is that kelp breaks easily. To avoid becoming tangled, keep your dive gear—fin straps, knives, and other tools—close to your body. Keep enough air in your tank to surface clear of the kelp. And always stay close to your dive partner, so he can help free you if snagged. If you must pass through kelp on the surface, do so by crawling and clearing a path in front of you. Most important, *relax.* Kelp is not attack trained. With careful, deliberate movements, kelp is easy to handle.

Hunting. California offers some of the best underwater hunting in the world. Succulent lobster, tender abalone, and game fish of all types can be gathered here. In all locations, strict game laws protect marine life. It's your responsibility to become familiar with the regulations and obtain the proper licenses. At local dive stores you can get information regarding fishing licenses and specific hunting regulations.

Dive Stores. There are many dive stores in Central California, but only a few are found along this stretch of coast. Bring everything you need with you. Some areas are quite remote.

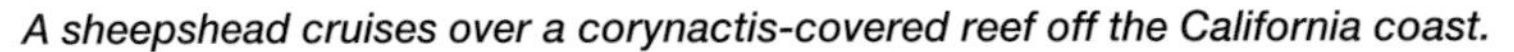

A sheepshead cruises over a corynactis-covered reef off the California coast.

2

Diving in Southern Monterey County: Big Sur's Coastline

Big Sur's remote rugged and steep shoreline is probably one of the most beautiful sites on the West Coast. Many spots are accessible, but they require long hikes down steep rocky cliffs with heavy scuba gear. Those divers who challenge the area will not be disappointed. Pristine and uncrowded coves with a plethora of colorful marine life abound. There is good news now for central coast divers looking for boat-based adventures. The *Pacific Star* runs multiday trips from Moss Landing to the most remote, inaccessible, and beautiful dive sites along the Big Sur coast. The *Princess* runs trips out of

Copper rockfish are found throughout the rocky reef system from the Ventura County line to Big Sur. The farther north a diver travels, the larger and more prolific these critters become.

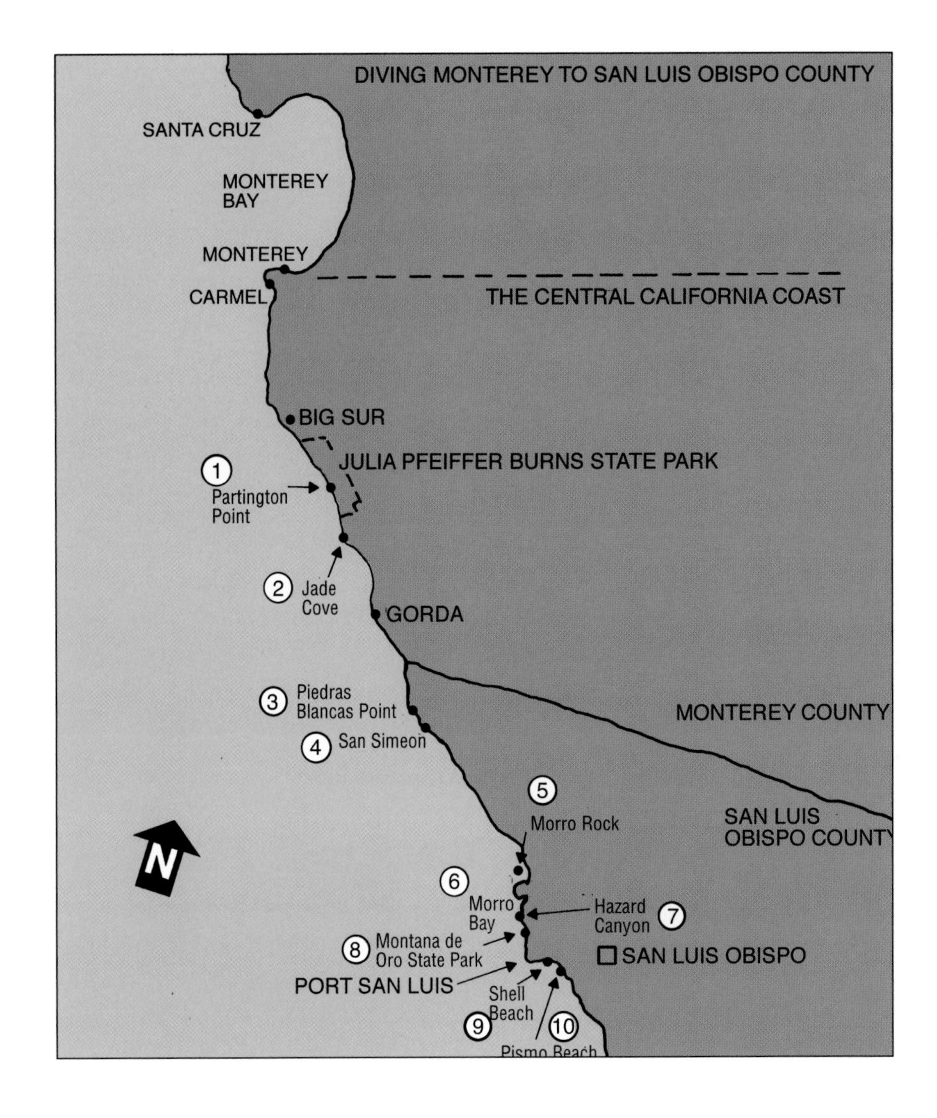

Morro Bay to Pt. Buchon, and the *Gray Finn* carries divers from Port San Luis as far north as San Simeon on single-to-five-day excursions. As dive vessels open these new regions, Central California divers are discovering a world of underwater resources heretofore completely unexplored.

Diving in this area should be attempted only when the weather is calm, even for advanced divers. Large swells, shallow reefs, and unpredictable wind and current can ruin your day if caution is not used. The payoff is that the Big Sur coast is wild and unpopulated and provides divers the freedom to explore seldom visited reefs and kelp beds. An extra plus is that even though visibility may be reduced, the abundance of colorful marine life is

Red abalone, the "Holy Grail" among seagoing gourmets, can still be taken from Yankee Point and southward along the central coast.

astounding. Here, the northern influence from British Columbia via the Humbolt current is readily seen. There are many colder water marine species to observe and enjoy.

If delectable red abalone is on your mind, remember these sea going delicacies may only be taken by free divers (no tanks) from Yankee Point northward.

Excellent rocky beach diving is available a short drive south of Monterey and Carmel. Just be sure to review surf and weather reports before you pack up the car on your road trip to Big Sur. Inclement weather can render the entire Big Sur coast dangerously undivable. When the weather is fair, however, plan on enjoying yourself. You are in for a treat. Some of the best beach diving during good conditions can be found at Partington Point and Jade Cove. And remember, if you are interested in boat diving this area, contact the *Pacific Star* for their schedule.

A diver carefully measures his abalone catch. Abalone must be measured on the bottom before placing them in a game bag. It's a good idea to double check the size at the surface. Fines for undersized abs are steep. ▶

Partington Point 1

Typical depth range:	20–90 feet
Access:	Steep road
Water entry:	Rocky
Snorkeling:	Not advised unless advanced free diver
Rating:	Advanced to ultra-advanced
Visibility:	20–30 feet or better

Located inside Julia Pfieffer Burns State Park, this is one of the few spots with relatively easy access in Big Sur. Camp sites are available within the park, as well as restroom and shower facilities. Partington is the only water entrance point within the park for divers. You may be able to make arrangements with park rangers to drive down a steep, rough road to unload your equipment, but even so, you'll still have some equipment hauling ahead to stage your gear for the dive.

This area is not often visited (about 100 divers a year make the attempt according to park officials) because of the risky rocky entry and exit point and exposed conditions to surf and wind. Park rangers recommend that only the very advanced dive Partington.

The Big Sur coastline is lush, pristine, and steep.

Schools of perch grace the waters at Partington Cove and elsewhere along the Central coast.

Risk aside, on a calm day, Partington makes an excellent dive site. A short distance offshore, rocky reefs, tunnels, and caves are home to spectacular varieties of anemones and rockfish. Cold water nudibranchs are found at Partington, as well as sea lions and the occasional sea otter. Some underwater caves transit the reef system, allowing divers to swim through to the other side. Partington features a large offshore kelp bed and good visibility. Water clarity is usually good, ranging from 20 to 50 feet or more.

As good as the diving at Partington can be, divers must pay close attention to sea conditions to safely explore the area.

Jade Cove 2

Typical depth range:	10–30 feet
Access:	Long, steep trail
Water entry:	Rocky and large pebbles
Snorkeling:	Fair
Rating:	Intermediate
Visibility:	10–20 feet

Located directly off Highway 1, south of Julia Pfieffer Burns State Park, Jade Cove, is appropriately named for the rocky treasures that can be gathered here. Years ago, the largest piece of jade (about the size of a small suitcase) was recovered by Al Tillman, NAUI Instructor #1. The piece has frequently been on display at the Los Angeles Natural History Museum. Even today, divers can return with fine specimens of this rare mineral—but they have to work for it.

Jade Cove is one of the most popular dive sites along the Central California coast.

The path leading from the highway toward the cliff trail at Jade Cove is a healthy hike for divers.

Divers access the area by hiking across a bluff and down a steep trail. The area is open to swells and current, and large waves frequently render the area undivable. On calmer days however, Jade Cove is a treasure to behold. Even without finding the exotic green stones, divers can explore lush kelp beds and photograph a variety of colorful rockfish, anemones, and occasional nudibranch. Spear fishermen frequent the area looking for large cabezon and ling cod. Because of the shallow relief of the cove, the water often surges, making divers "go with the flow" as they weave back and forth through the kelp and over the rocks in a constant sway of the ocean. Visibility is usually not as good as Partington.

While you're in the area, grab your road map and cruise over to Gorda, a small roadside town with a very impressive jade museum.

3

Diving San Luis Obispo County

Not as remote or inaccessible to beach divers as portions of the Big Sur coast, the area from Piedras Blancas to Pismo Beach is another beautiful stretch of California coastline. Still, rugged, but not as isolated, there are numerous areas for divers to frequent. Unlike the southern portions of the state, the water is colder, and marine life represents a northern influence found in British Columbia.

Here, beach divers will find rolling pastures stretching down to the water's edge, sandy beaches, and rugged rocky coastlines. The whole area is open to the effects of swell and weather, so be certain conditions are favorable before embarking on a scuba road trip.

San Luis Obispo County is a haven for surfers and sailboarders. Caution is advised in picking a dive area to avoid a hit and run collision with a large piece of fiberglass during entries and exits.

As sea otters continue to migrate southward, divers may encounter these frisky mammals, either on the surface lying on their backs eating shellfish or darting about underwater looking for more. The whole section from Piedras Blancas Point to San Simeon State Beach is a sea otter refuge.

Brightly colored spotted rose anemones are common among coastal reefs and in shallower waters.

Expect to see numerous California sea lions frolicking among the Central coast's kelp beds.

Some of the dive sites involve heavy surf entries and exits, but once out the diving is good, so pick your sites well and be sure they are commensurate with your diving ability. Morro Rock and Montana de Oro are good examples of great diving, but they afford a wild and wooly ride during entry and exit. San Luis Obispo County is a underwater wilderness compared to many other sites. It's hardy diving, but can be well worth the effort, and should be on every diver's underwater itinerary.

Piedras Blancas Point 3

Typical depth range:	10–40 feet
Access:	Park along Highway 1
Water entry:	Sand and rocky beach
Snorkeling:	Poor to fair
Rating:	Intermediate—advanced
Visibility:	10 to 20 feet

Approximately seven miles north of San Simeon is a curve and dip along Highway 1. The area is easy to notice because of the usual parking melee of trucks and vans carrying sailboarders that line up on either side of the road. Park, walk down the small bluff, and be welcomed to Piedras Blancas Point. A small lighthouse rests to the north. The sailboarders launch from the beach and race around the offshore rocks near the lighthouse at the northern end of the point and jump waves along the outer reefs. For divers, this should not be a problem if you keep an eye on the sailboard's coming and going. Divers and sailboarders can peacefully coexist in this area. The good news is when the wind is blowing 30 knots and the surf is up, diving is not

A diver returns from a night dive. Note the pelagic red crabs (also called tuna crabs) in the surrounding water. These invertebrates spend their entire lives drifting at sea and occasionally wash up along California beaches.

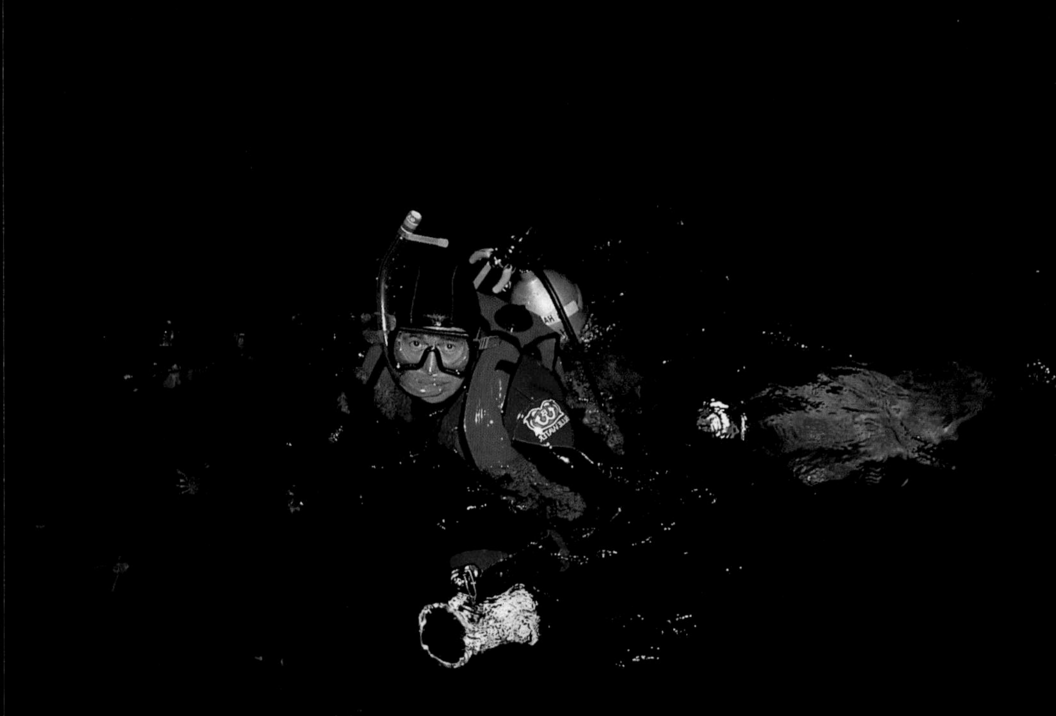

Rockfish become more common and grow in larger profusion the farther north one travels along the Central California coast.

a good idea anyway, but the sailboarders are exciting to watch and photograph from the surface, and the beach is excellent for a breezy picnic lunch. Piedras Blancas is a very picturesque portion of the California coastline.

When the wind is calm and swells subside, Piedras Blancas is a "sleeper" dive destination. Enter the water slightly north of the parking area, and you'll soon find yourself in rocky reef areas with interspersed patches of eel grass. The area is large and offers a lot of ground to cover, making it a site that can be dived numerous times without seeing it all. It is an excellent area for underwater photographers looking for nudibranchs, anemones, seastars, and other invertebrates. Hunters often seek cabezon and other rockfish.

Piedras Blancas does not disappoint. Just be sure you tackle it on a calm day. High surf and currents can take some of the fun out of the expedition.

Rocky reef areas with small kelp beds inundate the area. And if you are really lucky, you'll find docile wolf eels and leopard sharks here. If dungeness crabs are on your dinner menu, you'll find them here as well. On good weather days, Piedras Blancas reveals a well kept secret for divers, a secret that the central coast unveils on special occasions.

San Simeon Point 4

Typical depth range:	20–40 feet
Access:	Enter off Highway 1 near San Simeon Rd
Water entry:	Sand and rocks
Snorkeling:	Good
Rating:	Intermediate
Visibility:	10–30 feet

This area was originally part of Rancho San Simeon and later used as a whaling station in 1864. George Hearst bought the rancho in 1865 and constructed a wharf facility for trading and exporting. The area is now part of William Randolph Hearst Memorial State Beach (Hearst Castle State Historical Monument is located in the mountains above the sea).

Divers can enter near the fishing pier facility and park. Where they go from there is up to them. The sheltered cove by the pier is considered the last protected anchorage for mariners south of San Francisco. Consequently, diving inside this point is usually calm on the north end of the beach. The area is predominantly sandy, but there are a few rocky reefs with kelp beds. The terrain shifts to a rockier area near the point. Divers can make the long swim there or take a long walk along the beach and enter the water. There is a good area to look for rockfish, halibut, and cabezon, and sea otters can be observed lounging in the kelp beds eating shellfish.

Incredible varieties of strange invertebrates, such as these sea stars, are found along Central California's rocky reef systems.

Colorful bright yellow anemones can often be found on deep water reefs.

The cove and point at San Simeon provide divers with a large protected area to explore and enjoy. Whether searching the sandy flats for halibut or photographing colorful anemones on the low lying reefs, there are an abundance of activities to pursue. The facilities in the area include picnic sites, restrooms, and lots of available parking. The pier provides fishing access and dive boat charters. Check the *Gray Finn's* charter schedule. Occasionally the boat is in San Simeon picking up or dropping off divers who have been exploring the coast from Pt. Buchon to San Simeon. Even if you are not diving, San Simeon is a great place to visit. Strolling along the pine trees near the water's edge is a relaxing experience.

Morro Rock 5

Typical depth range:	20–40 feet
Access:	Enter off Highway 1 near the PG & E Plant
Water entry:	Rocky
Snorkeling:	Fair
Rating:	Advanced
Visibility:	5–15 feet

This is a 576-foot volcanic rock rising like a monolith above the sea, west of Morro Bay. A causeway runs between the bay and the rock, allowing a view of the water on both sides while you drive to the parking area. Park in the dirt lot by the restrooms (in the shadow of Morro Rock). A secondary parking lot is adjacent to the breakwater at Morro Bay. Diving Morro Bay is not for everyone because of the extreme water conditions. Diving in the shadow of Morro Rock offers good swell protection, but occasionally big waves roll through. The surf gets quite large at Morro Rock, making it a haven for surfers. Each year, boats (and occasionally lives) are lost at the harbor entrance to the south. Never dive Morro Rock if surf is larger than three feet. Swells can pick up rapidly and without warning. It is not uncommon for larger "sneaker" sets of waves to roar in cresting eight feet or larger. Choose your diving day at Morro Rock wisely and evaluate conditions carefully.

Diving at Morro Rock is awe-inspiring and challenging. At the north base of the rock, PG & E has a warm-water discharge channel that flows quickly seaward. Divers can enter at this point and get a free ride out to their dive site, but will not be able to exit at the same place. Exiting involves a long swim towards land outside of the PG&E outflow. Divers cannot enter and exit at the same point.

As the current slackens, moving away from the entry point, divers can descend into an area where sand and rock meet. There is a lot of eel grass growing here. The water quickly becomes cold, and divers will find large metridium and green anemones, tunicates, sponge, and varieties of rockfish. It is a good area for spearfishing if you feel like swimming your catch all the way into the beach. Sea otters can be observed here as well, presenting unique photographic opportunities.

The waters at Morro Rock can be hazardous if conditions are not evaluated properly. ►

Morro Bay 6

Typical depth range: 15–35 feet
Access: Inside harbor, dirt roadside
Water entry: Rocky
Snorkeling: Fair
Rating: Novice
Visibility: 6–15 feet

Located along the southern side of the causeway leading out to Morro Rock is Morro Bay's Harbor, designed and built by the U.S. Army Corps of Engineers. Here, next to several large rocks at the fringe of the parking lot is an area where divers climb a small flight of rocks to get into the water. Water conditions here are usually dead-flat calm. In fact, most diving instructors in this area often use the resources found inside Morro Bay as a training site for students.

But "divability" has its price. Calm waters abound for sure, but the marine life found inside Morro Bay, although interesting, is nothing compared to more open and unprotected parts of the coast.

Inside Morro Bay, divers will encounter a small kelp bed. Perch, large dungenous and spider crabs, sea urchins, anemones, and other colorful invertebrates. Occasionally, sea otter swim along the surface and munch on shellfish.

Visibility is marginal, but it's usually adequate for training dives. When conditions on the outside are calmer, visibility is improved by comparison. Even though water clarity in Morro Bay may not always be at a tropical best, it's always nice to know there usually is a spot where diving is guaranteed.

Morro Bay is also the place to catch the dive boat *Princess* for longer range excursions for divers along the Central California coast.

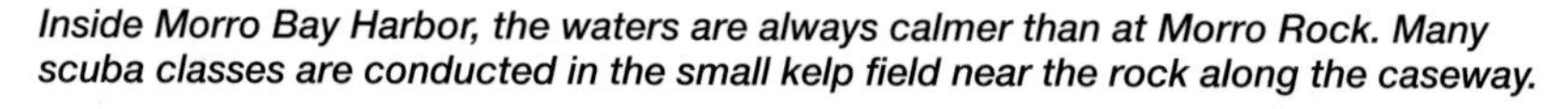

Inside Morro Bay Harbor, the waters are always calmer than at Morro Rock. Many scuba classes are conducted in the small kelp field near the rock along the caseway.

Hazard Canyon 7

Typical depth range:	20–40 feet
Access:	Dirt trail
Water entry:	Rocky
Snorkeling:	Fair
Rating:	Intermediate–advanced
Visibility:	10–20 feet

Hidden in a grove of eucalyptus trees on the road to Montana de Oro State Park, Hazard Canyon is a secret spot among locals. Take Los Osos Valley Road to Pecho Valley Road and you are on your way. There are no signs announcing Hazard Canyon's entrance—just a bend in the eucalyptus-lined road and two or three cars parked on the side by the trail. It takes a bit of a walk to get to, so bear this in mind when preparing to haul your equipment to the beach. Once on shore, you'll discover the effort was worthwhile. Usually unpopulated, this remote site features a table-top reef system with smaller rocky reefs and kelp scattered between the coarse sandy bottom. Diving Hazards should only be attempted on days when the swell is small, or you'll find yourself sharing the area with the central coast surfing population.

Spanish shawl (flabellinopsis iodena) *is just one of many varieties of nudibranch found off the central coast's beaches.*

Bright tube anemone plumes extend from their lairs among the sandy plains.

The area is a gold mine for marine life. Whether you want to spear a rockfish or cabezon for dinner or take advantage of the myriads of photographic opportunities available, Hazard Canyon will not disappoint. Large green and purple anemones flourish, as well as sea hares, nudibranchs, and species of rockfish. If divers are fortunate, they may encounter 20- to 25-foot basking sharks in the open water areas beyond the shallow reef areas when a plankton bloom is present.

Surge and current are usually the order of the day at Hazards, so pick a favorable tide and plan your dive accordingly. A good diver will evaluate conditions carefully before jumping in. Hazard Canyon is a memorable dive site. The area is relatively pristine and its remote location along the bluffs beyond the eucalyptus trees provide a view of California found in years gone by. Quiet solitude and uncrowded conditions make this an enjoyable area to visit as well as dive.

Montana de Oro Beach 8

Typical depth range:	10–30 feet
Access:	Public parking then sandy beach
Water entry:	Rocky or sandy
Snorkeling:	Good
Rating:	Advanced
Visibility:	10–20 feet

It's hard to miss the entrance to Montana de Oro State Park. It's a dead end on Pecho Valley Road, a few miles south of Hazard Canyon and Morro Bay. The coarse sandy beach contains lots of small pieces of jade for mineral collectors. There are two good areas of access: one directly in front of the parking area in the cove, and the other slightly north in the rocky channels that are characteristic of the area. The channels allow divers to ride the

A diver inspects the ledge beneath a kelp bed for a potential abalone dinner.

Corynactis and metridium anemones are found on some of the deeper current-fed reefs.

outgoing surge seaward, or divers may opt for a rocky entry depending on conditions. As with most of California's central coast areas, there is little protection from swell, current, and wind. Surf conditions at Montana de Oro may range from calm to ferocious. It's a good idea to watch the incoming swells for half an hour to get a feel for the wave action. Diving the area at slack high tide is a good idea.

Like Hazard Canyon, Montana de Oro features a variety of colorful anemones, rockfish, ling cod, cabezon, and abalone and dungeness crab to boot. Colorful varieties of sea stars and other invertebrates offer good photographic opportunities although rough conditions can keep many photographers at bay. The area is not very deep, but rocky reefs are literally everywhere, making it a fun, surge-filled dive. Offshore Montana de Oro is actually an extension of Hazard Canyon Reef, but it offers easier access and more interesting terrain.

Underwater, divers will encounter sea stacks, tiny islands of volcanic rock standing alone as miniature pinnacles when wave action and erosion separated them from the mainland. There are numerous surge channels in the area, allowing divers to explore shallow underwater canyons.

Shell Beach 9

Typical depth range:	20–45 feet
Access:	Exit off Highway 1
Water entry:	Sand and rocky beach
Snorkeling:	Fair to good
Rating:	Novice–Intermediate
Visibility:	15 to 35 feet

Shell Beach is a small protected cove located north of Pismo and south of Avila Beaches, near the entrance to San Luis Obispo Bay and Port San Luis. The area is plainly visible from Pacific Coast Highway and is resplendent with thick kelp beds at the base of a small bluff. The small mesa overlooking the site is a favorite stopping area for afternoon picnickers, travelers wanting to get out of their cars and stretch their legs, and "otter-watchers" with binoculars, who roam the bluffs observing the antics of sea otters lounging in the kelp. A short climb down a trail leads divers onto the beach. The intermittent patches of exposed rocky reef and sand make Shell Beach an excellent area to observe tidepool marine life. It is an ideal home to anemones, crabs, small fish, and the occasional octopus.

The colorful plumes of the tube anemone are found in the underwater sand of most California beaches. They make excellent macro subjects.

Lingcod are a favorite quarry for coastal spear fishermen.

Once divers pack their gear down from the bluff, there is plenty of room to suit up along the sandy beach and to enter the water. The best entries are made in the sandy channels between rocks. A short swim from shore will place divers in the kelp beds among the fish and reefs. Starting in 15 feet of water and venturing seaward towards 40 feet, divers will encounter varieties of rockfish, ling cod, abalone, scallops, numerous anemones, and sea stars.

As with most areas along the central coast, weather and sea conditions are factors to consider before diving in. The good news is that Point Buchon (a large promontory south of Montana de Oro) forms protection from incoming north and northwesterly swells. This means that Shell Beach is often calm enough to dive when other areas may not be. This protected location also tends to receive more sunny and clear weather than other spots nearby. San Luis Obispo Creek empties in the ocean between Shell Beach and Port San Luis. Depending on the outflow of water into the ocean, fine sediment can drift to Shell Beach and reduce water clarity. Perhaps the only good aspect of California's occasional drought cycle is that the creek often resembles a trickle of water and does not usually impact visibility at Shell Beach. When the drought periods end expect this to change.

Overall, Shell Beach offers good diving and reasonable beach access compared to other Central California sites where divers scale steep cliffs to establish a beachhead.

Pismo State Beach 10

Typical depth range:	5–50 feet
Access:	Parking on the sand, Exit Hwy 1
Water entry:	Sandy beach
Snorkeling:	Fair
Rating:	Intermediate
Visibility:	15 to 25 feet

The Chumash Indians called Pismo Beach "pismu" because of the natural tar that seeps through fissures in the sea floor off the central coast (often washing ashore on the beach). This tar was used to pitch the hulls of plank board canoes and to make watertight baskets. In the early 1900s, Pismo Beach became a favorite spot for vacationers.

Probably the most famous legacy of the area is the large "Pismo" clams. By the end of World War II, 100,000 tons of the large clams were harvested annually by commercial clammers. Recreational clammers, equipped with hip boots and pitch forks waded out into the surf and harvested more. Today the sport limit for Pismo clams is ten per day because this resource has become markedly reduced with the comeback of California's sea otter population. Sea otters (and overzealous clammers) have almost exhausted the clam supply. Divers often visit Pismo State Beach to help themselves to clams by scooting along the shallows with an abalone iron and extracting these delicious bivalves from the sand.

Sunsets at Pismo Beach can be spectacular. Divers can camp along the shore near the sand dunes.

Seemingly an underwater desert, Pismo Beach provides divers with encounters with marine life from the sand squadron. Shovelnose shark, rays, flounder, halibut, and corbina are often sought after by spearfishermen as well. Divers should be careful to avoid getting "hooked" by the numerous surf fishers that cast their lines out into the breakers. Because the beach slopes gradually to deeper depths, divers can bypass this nuisance by conducting their forays in ten feet of water or deeper. Pismo is quite shallow close to shore.

Pismo is the only beach in Central and Southern California where visitors are allowed to drive automobiles onto the hard-packed sand. Non-fourwheel drive vehicles should steer clear of the softer sand near the dunes that flank the highwater mark, and should avoid venturing too close to the water. Several cars a year get stuck in the wet sand, and the incoming tides submerge the vehicles. Stick to the main thoroughfare, and you'll be fine.

A wilderness camping area is located at the extreme southern end of the beach. The only facilities are portable restrooms, and campers must pack out all trash in bags provided by park rangers. Back your vehicle all the way beyond the hightide mark—otherwise you might emerge from your camper to find your barbecue, chairs, and lantern have all washed away. Pismo Beach is a great diving area. The benefits of close overnight camping and the ability to park a few yards away from your dive site are extra bonuses. And if you are lucky enough to bag some clams (California fishing license required), a clambake or chioppino stew made over a campfire is a great way to end a day of diving.

Sea palms and perch are a common sight in California intertidal water surge zones.

4

Diving in Santa Barbara County

From the Nipomo Sand Dunes where the Santa Maria River trickles into the sea, to remote ranch land near Pt. Conception, Santa Barbara County displays a mixture of central coast serenity and unspoiled beauty. The Santa Barbara coast offers a quick and convenient getaway from the crowds found further south and many excellent diving opportunities a short distance away from Highways 1 and 101.

A significant portion of this area—Vandenberg Air Force Base—is unaccessible to the general public. This sprawling complex extends from the southern end of Point Sal to Jalama Creek. Vandenberg is the site of numerous Pacific missile launches, where triton rockets are fired thousands of miles to target sites within the Pacific Missile Range. At one time, Vandenberg was considered an alternative launch site for the space shuttle. Today, only the Vandenberg Air Force Base Dive Club can access the numerous but often

Gorgonian fans come in a variety of hues. Divers will find a variety of them along the Santa Barbara coast.

California spiny lobster are still encountered along the rocky reefs at The Ranch and southward. These species become harder to find north of Jalama Beach Park.

rough dive sites along this deserted part of the coast. From Vandenberg south to Gaviota, coastal access is also limited because of private land holdings, such as the Bixby and Hollister ranches near Point Conception. This part of the California coast is often only viewed by Amtrak passengers riding the rails from Los Angeles to San Francisco.

There is one notable exception for diving access into the area from Pt. Conception to Gaviota, and that is access by small boat.

Diving the Ranch: A launching ramp exists on the beach at Surf, the last public coastal access north of Lompoc. There is also a sling located on the pier at Gaviota. Either way, small inflatables and fixed hull vessels can be launched locally allowing divers to visit "The Ranch." The Ranch is a series of private holdings on some of the most beautiful and exclusive coastal areas along the west coast. Kelp beds are prolific here and reefs are numerous. Almost any where a thick kelp patch is floating, good diving can be guaranteed. Because The Ranch is not often visited by divers (with the exception of commercial fishermen) huge abalone still wait to be collected. Lobster divers and spearfishermen seeking rockfish will not be disappointed at The Ranch. Anchoring a small boat up inside the kelp beds is often advisable.

For those of us without boats, most diving access from shore begins south of the Santa Ynez Valley at Gaviota Beach.

Once divers get closer to the city of Santa Barbara, coastal access to the reefs and offshore kelp beds becomes more available for beach divers. Yet some of the best diving lies within the Air Force Base environs, including the wreckage of seven U.S. Navy destroyers that ran aground at Point Arguello in 1923 (see *Pisces Guide to Southern California Shipwrecks*). When missiles are not flying, these sites are available by boat.

◀ A diver explores a small colorful reef at The Ranch, north of Gaviota State Beach.

Point Sal State Beach 11

Typical depth range:	50–80 feet
Access:	Exit Hwy 1 at Brown Rd West. Sometimes restricted due to missile launch at Vandenberg
Water entry:	Rock and sandy beach
Snorkeling:	Not recommended
Rating:	Advanced
Visibility:	15–35 feet

Want to really get away from it all? Take the Brown Exit off Pacific Coast Highway (US 1) and head west through a zigzagging and unkept road toward the ocean. The road actually crosses Vandenberg Air Force Base property, and is closed during missile launches. Determine accessibility before you drive in by calling (805) 733-3717. The road is not in the best of shape, and can often be undrivable after winter storms.

The sun rises along Santa Barbara coast. There are many excellent dive sites here, and the cliffs are markedly less steep than those found along Big Sur.

Bright red rose anemones like this one represent just one of many species found just a short distance off California's beaches.

But to those who bide their time and make the journey, a reward awaits. This is California as it was when George Vancouver charted its coast. A trading wharf, no longer in existence, was built during the 1800s to export grain from the Santa Ynez Valley. The ridge of Point Sal itself is believed to have originated in the mid-Pacific over 125 million years ago and moved to its present position because of violent shifts in the earth's crust. Pillow lavas are commonly found in the area.

Divers will find the underwater terrain unique and diverse, with well-defined reef systems interspersed with sand and kelp. Abalone and scallops grow thick in the intertidal areas. You may encounter large California or monstrous Pacific halibut in the sand flats. The southern end of the beach is a haul-out area for sea lion and harbor seals.

Currents can be unpredictable in this area, and strong swells can batter the rocky promontories. Because of Point Sal's secluded nature, divers should be extra cautious. Should an emergency arise, help will not be close at hand.

But for those who have a yen to explore a "wilder side" of the south central coast, Point Sal should be on your underwater "hit list."

Jalama Beach County Park 12

Typical depth range:	15–40 feet
Access:	Exit Hwy 1 at Jalama Rd (SW)
Water entry:	Sandy beach
Snorkeling:	Fair
Rating:	Intermediate
Visibility:	10–25 feet

Named after Jalama Creek, which empties into the Pacific, this secluded county park offers campsites, restrooms, and parking facilities. The park is five miles north of Point Conception and encompasses 28 acres. Jalama Road meanders across the creek several times as it switches back amidst a rural area featuring California black walnut, maple, and huckleberry trees. Jalama is truly one of the prettiest sites along this section of coast.

Jalama features two distinct reef systems: an offshore finger reef that protects the calmer intertidal areas and small rocky outcroppings. This outer reef has been a favorite surf spot for years and is now a favorite haunt for windsurfers. When the surf is calm and the wind is slack, water clarity can become surprisingly clear, revealing abalone, scallops, anemones, and Pismo clams in the sand flats. Today, Jalama is an excellent area for diving when conditions are favorable.

Because of its user-friendly access and its attractive campsite, Jalama is a great place for a scuba safari. Bring a tent, some good friends, and extra tanks or a compressor, and enjoy fresh abalone or rockfish around a roaring campfire. Like Point Sal, Jalama is still off the beaten track, although much more accessible.

Metridiums make graceful, beautiful subjects for underwater photography. Divers will find them on deeper water reefs along the Big Sur Coast.

Corynactis like this can often be found in the shallow reefs.

Typical depth range:	15–40 feet
Access:	Exit Hwy 101 as it turns inland. Use Gaviota offramp
Water entry:	Sandy beach with some rocks
Snorkeling:	Fair
Rating:	Novice–intermediate
Visibility:	10–20 feet

There are ample facilities at Gaviota State park, including newly constructed picnic areas. The 5½ miles of shoreline where Gaviota Creek runs seaward feature day-use facilities as well as campsites. Hikers will enjoy Gaviota Canyon, which rambles inland. The creek, lined with dense riprarian woodland, supports a small and sporadic steelhead salmon run. The remnants of an ancient Chumash village have been excavated along the beach by archaeologists, and it is believed that Juan Rodriguez Cabrillo stopped here for supplies during his exploration of the California coastline.

Gaviota Pier is a popular site for fishermen, and there is a small sling to launch inflatables and other small boats from the pier. Here, surfers and divers can gain access to The Ranch. There are several small reefs that fringe the area, and kelp often grows in abundance. Divers enter the waters from the sandy beach and snorkel to the kelp beds. Divers can encounter lobster, abalone, rockfish, anemones, and sea stars on the reefs. Sand'dabs, bat rays, halibut, and clams may be found in the sand.

The area is not often dived because visibility is usually not the best in the area. But if you don't mind less than tremendous water clarity, Gaviota is a great place to camp, dive, and have a good time. A short hike in the canyon reveals a hot natural sulphur spring.

The scenery is breathtaking between Gaviota Pier north to The Ranch.

Here are some of the untapped treasures near Jalama Beach Park. Many varieties and colors of anemones abound in the area.

Tajiguas 14

Typical depth range:	45 feet
Access:	Dirt path off Hwy 101
Water entry:	Sandy beach
Snorkeling:	Good
Rating:	Novice–intermediate
Visibility:	15–35 feet

It's easy to understand why diving and other leisure activities abound at the state beaches along the coast slightly north of Santa Barbara. The state beaches offer excellent facilities, including restrooms, camping, showers, and food service. But expect large crowds. To escape the crowds and enjoy fine diving, try Tajiguas.

A series of rocky ledges lie directly off the beach and extend to the west. The ledges begin in shallow water and run parallel to shore to depths of 40 feet. Most of the rocks are low-lying, rising 3–5 feet from the bottom. Despite their low profile, some of the ledges extend out five feet, creating large overhangs. This is an excellent area for macrophotography. You may find clumps of yellow, pink, and lavender corynactis anemones, as well as white-spotted rose anemones, with vivid red bodies and tentacles, and large

Look closely when you inspect the reef systems here so you won't miss the small crabs camouflaged atop the rocks.

Kelp bass, also known as calico bass, are a favorite quarry among spear fishermen.

rose anemones, characterized by white tentacles and a deep red body. A small community of red, brown, and California golden gorgonians can be discovered on the deeper reefs. Also expect to find the brilliant orange and blue Spanish shawl and white and gold horned nudibranchs.

Fish are a little sparse in the area, but look under the rock ledges for rockfish and around the kelp beds for game fish. Abalone and lobster are also present, though the area has been worked over heavily by game seekers. Scallops can be found on reefs in deep-water areas that are somewhat inaccessible from shore.

Entry to the beach is on the south side of Highway 101. Parking and access are not visible from the north-bound lanes. If you're traveling northbound on Highway 101, turn around at the gas station located approximately two miles north of Refugio State Beach. Park next to the highway on the dirt areas. A dirt path across the railroad tracks leads to the beach. There usually are one or more vehicles parked by the tracks to help mark the spot. The path is safe and easy to travel, even with heavy gear. There are no facilities on the beach or near the parking areas.

The best diving and entry can be found at the west end of the beach. Surfers congregate at the eastern end. Although the beach is sandy, there are cobblestones in the surf, particularly in the winter. There is also access farther west on the road that leads to the west side of the point. The incline is steep and sometimes treacherous, but it shortens the swim to the outer kelp areas.

Water conditions at Tajiguas are usually good. Thanks to a mild current, visibility is often better than at beaches farther south, averaging 10 feet. Try it during the summer when swells are slack. Visibility improves during these months.

Refugio State Beach 15

Typical depth range:	10–40 feet
Access:	Park entrance off Hwy 101
Water entry:	Sandy beach
Snorkeling:	Good
Rating:	Novice–intermediate
Visibility:	15–35 feet

Probably the most picturesque State Park between Santa Barbara and Gaviota, Refugio is nestled in a small wooded valley, complete with streams, biking and hiking trails, and easy beach access. Refugio Beach beckons the leisure diver. The secluded beach, dotted with majestic palm trees, is a perfect spot for an afternoon picnic. There are also excellent camping facilities including 109 campsites, restrooms, showers, and eateries, plus good diving. In fact, you could have a terrific time without even getting wet. But if good diving is what you had in mind, you've come to the right place.

Refugio State Beach is located approximately 25 miles north of Santa Barbara off Highway 101. Turn off the highway at the ramp marked Refugio Beach and follow the signs. Once through the gate, you'll pass under railroad tracks. Turn right for the northwest end of the beach; turn right for the southeast beach. There's ample parking close to the water's edge, but there is a fee for entering the park.

This picnic area at Refugio State Beach is a popular after-dive eatery site among the wet suit crowd.

A ten footer "steams" through El Capitan's northern point during a big winter swell. This is one reason why El Cap is a better dive site in the spring and summer months.

Reefs and kelp lie 50 yards from shore. The variety of terrain and sea life is sure to delight divers at all levels. At the southeast end of the beach near the camping area, kelp beds line a rocky bottom. Just 20 feet deep, this is an excellent area for snorkeling, particularly in calm weather. Beyond the kelp are a series of jagged rock ledges that run parallel to shore. The ledges rise 12 feet from the bottom in some spots, creating overhangs that attract unusual species of marine life. Look on the ledges for nudibranchs and on the sandy bottom for sea mice. Anemones lend a splash of color to the reefs, and sea hares (sea slugs) are everywhere.

The kelp beds attract few game fish, and those that can be found—such as the kelp bass—scare easily and are difficult to approach. You won't find any abalone near the reefs at the eastern side of the beach. If hunting is your thing, you'll have better luck along the coast toward the northwest and around the small point.

In this area, kelp is attached to low-lying reefs in 15–25 feet of water. In some places you'll discover an occasional abalone or lobster. This area is best suited to divers who are in good physical condition because it's a long swim from the beach. Nearby reefs can be reached by inflatable boat, which you can launch from the beach in calm weather. Parking is situated a few yards from the beach. And, although the beach is somewhat protected from rough conditions coming out of the northwest, it's a good idea to check conditions ahead of time.

The only drawback to diving Refugio State Beach is the summer crowds. If you plan to camp during your stay, be sure to make reservations early in the season.

El Capitan State Beach 16

Typical depth range:	10–40 feet
Access:	Park entrance from Hwy 101
Water entry:	Sandy beach or boulders
Snorkeling:	Good
Rating:	Intermediate
Visibility:	10–30 feet

"El Cap" as it's commonly referred to by those who frequent the area, is another excellent state beach with great access. If you liked Refugio, you'll like El Capitan, which is nestled in a pretty canyon with dense foliage. When visiting on holiday weekends, make your campsite reservations well in advance. This holds true with any of the "camping beaches" along the California coast. You can make reservations by contacting directory assistance for the beach you are interested in. If one beach is full, try another; you may get lucky.

Visibility is reasonable here, but even if water clarity is less than spectacular, the diving terrain and abundance of marine life make up for it. The profusion of shallow water anemones truly make this a photographer's playground. Other brightly hued invertebrates and nudibranchs are not uncommon in the area. The best diving is along a small point to the south by the picnic and barbecue areas.

The terrain of shallow rocky finger reefs, sand, and boulders is similar to what may be encountered at Refugio to the north. Lush kelp is often prevalent in the southern area, and during bug season an unwary lobster or two can be pulled out from its rocky lair for a campsite barbecue. Scallops and varieties of abalone are found here as well. El Capitan is another great coastal access area providing excellent facilities for a day trip, or a weekend camp out.

Because El Capitan Creek flows from the hills toward the sea, this area was a favorite spot for early Chumash inhabitants. Early coastal explorers obtained fresh water here as well. A significant Chumash village site was excavated by archeologists in the late 1950s.

El Cap deserves one word of warning however: Stay clear of the east and western promontories during periods of high south westerly swell. The area provides some of the best winter surfing along the coast with eight to twelve foot waves. If this is the case, leave your tanks at home and wax up the surfboard.

Naples Reef 17

Typical depth range: 20–55 feet
Access: Sandy beach
Water entry: Sandy beach (400-yd. snorkel to reef)
Snorkeling: Good for hardy skin divers
Rating: Advanced
Visibility: 20–50 feet
Note: Long surface swim, but worth it!

Many consider Naples Reef to be a boat dive, but nonetheless, it is often assaulted from the beach for one reason: it's one of Santa Barbara County's coastal best! Located off Highway 101 near Naples Point, the reef is a pinnacle rising from deep water slightly southwest of Ellwood Pier. Naples Reef has long been considered a fishermen's hot spot, receiving a large weekly contingent of commercial, sport, and private fishing craft. Commercial urchin and abalone divers have harvested the area heavily over the years, but there is more to Naples Reef than just the game it has to offer.

The terrain is diverse with small pinnacles, rocky reefs, sand patches, thick kelp, and schools of fish. Colorful anemones are common, so don't forget to

Colorful sea fans can be found at Naples Reef in Santa Barbara.

Sea palms become more common atop rocky shallows the farther north one ventures along the Central California coast.

bring your camera. Additionally, divers will find iridescent varieties of sea stars, nudibranchs, and anemones. Large specimens of sheephead, calico bass, rockfish, blacksmith, and varieties of perch frequent Naples regularly.

Because of its distance from shore, a little bit of oceanic influence is often present in the schools of Pacific barracuda and occasional white sea bass. For the hardy diver, Naples Reef is worth the swim.

Arroyo Burro Beach County Park 18

Typical depth range:	10–45 feet
Access:	Cliff Drive, North of Santa Barbara City
Water entry:	Sand and rock surf entry
Snorkeling:	Fair
Rating:	Novice to intermediate
Visibility:	10–15 feet

Near the Santa Barbara city limits, Arroyo Burro State Beach offers perhaps the best diving and the easiest access in Southern California. Arroyo Burro is neatly tucked into a small canyon about four miles north of Santa Barbara Harbor. Facilities include picnic tables, restrooms, and a small restaurant and snack bar. Local dive instructors use this site for check-out dives.

A diver explores a colorful reef along the Central California coast.

A diver comes face-to-face with a bright white metridium anemone.

The best diving is to the south of South Point. Getting to the Point requires some walking, but the sandy beach makes it a pleasant stroll. The bottom is mostly sand directly off the beach. But approximately 25–50 yards offshore of the Point, a series of rock ledges begin in 10–15 feet of water. Look under these ledges for colorful anemones, nudibranchs, and other invertebrates. Garibaldi, lingcod, sheepshead, calico bass, and halibut are also present.

Divers headed for Mohawk Reef often enter here. A large reef structure, Mohawk begins at South Point and extends south past Mesa Lane beach. However, the best dive spots on this reef are a long swim out. And because of the location of the reef, the best visibility is to the south, averaging 15 feet.

Mesa Lane and Mohawk Reef 19

Typical depth range:	15–40 feet
Access:	Cliff Drive to Mesa Lane
Water entry:	Rock and sand entry at base of cliff
Snorkeling:	Good for the dedicated
Rating:	Intermediate–advanced
Visibility:	10–15 feet

As you'll soon realize, finding clear waters along the Santa Barbara coast isn't always easy. At Mesa Lane, though, a reef makes this dive site one of the best in the county for sightseeing and photography.

Until recently, diving here was limited to boats or sure-footed divers who could negotiate the steep, treacherous path that led to the beach. This path has since been replaced by a staircase, albeit long and steep. But at least you can leave your hiking boots home!

Divers venturing to the Central California coast should be trained for surge conditions that are common and often tumultuous.

Sea stars are a popular target for up-close and personal photographs.

You get an excellent view of the diving area from the top of the stairway. There are a number of entry and exit points on the rock-strewn sandy beach. Offshore, kelp beds mark the best reefs, including Mohawk Reef, which extends in sections from north to south.

A small reef line begins within 25–50 yards of shore and extends in both directions along the coast. Much of the kelp you see 50–100 yards beyond the reef is new. Much of the kelp on the reef was destroyed years ago.

Small caves, huge rocks, large ledges, and overhangs are among common features. The reef rises about 15 feet above the bottom, which varies from 25–30 feet in depth. Depths drop to 40 feet just outside the kelp.

Fleshy sea pens are usually found in the colder northern waters, but on occasion a diver may come across one in the sand off Central California beaches.

Shoreline Park/Santa Cruz Street 20

Typical depth range:	10–25 feet
Access:	Off Shoreline Drive
Water entry:	"1,000 Steps" to beach
Snorkeling:	Fair
Rating:	Intermediate
Visibility:	15–30 feet

These two areas are closely situated, and the terrain and geography are similar in nature. The park is situated on a tall marine terrace. A 14-acre grassy bluff is a popular whale watching spot as gray whales migrate up and down the California coast. Interestingly, the bluff face was created by the Mesa Fault, which in 1925 almost leveled the city of Santa Barbara. Because of this recent tectonic activity, this area affords interesting underwater terrain for those willing to "hoof it" down the bluff to the beach.

Like many of the beach dive sites north of Santa Barbara proper, Shoreline Park is interspersed with sand flats and rocky reefs. There is however a large rocky reef system approximately 200 yards from shore with smaller finger reefs and sand in between. Kelp is sparse here, but divers will encounter halibut, rockfish, nudibranchs, and a complement of vibrant anemones.

Wolf eels, usually a colder water creature may be encountered along the deeper reefs in Central California.

5

Diving in Ventura County

Compared to other areas off the Southern California coast, Ventura county beaches are not a place divers traditionally throng to. That's what makes the area a pleasant surprise. There is more to the picture than meets the eye.

Visibility is usually on the lower end of the scale, and the region is often open to the effects of wind and swell, making it traditionally an area frequented by surfers rather than divers—or so it seems. For those who don't mind visibility lower than the spectacular Channel Islands a short boat ride from shore, there are a few sites they can enjoy immensely. So if an island adventure is not in the cards for you, the dive sites off Ventura County offer easy access, photographic and game opportunities, and decent underwater scenery, even if visibility is not always the best. Rincon Point, a famous surfing spot, starts at the Ventura/Santa Barbara county line. Water clarity is usually poor here. Run-off from Ventura River does little to help this. But moving slightly southward, there are a few "secret spots" (only secret to those who don't dive there) affording reasonable visibility, small crowds, and good facilities—not to mention a great sampling of California marine critters to observe and enjoy.

Summer months are usually an excellent time for divers to visit Ventura beaches since large surf occurs predominantly in the winter. From Mussel Shoals to Silver Strand Beach lies a wide expanse of coast often dotted with kelp beds far from shore. The snorkeling distance involved and general lack of visibility sends most divers boatward to the Channel Islands, even though the sand flats are often good hunting grounds for California halibut. The good news is there are several somewhat consistent exceptions: Emma Wood State Park, La Jennelle Park, Deer Creek Road, and Sycamore Cove State Park.

The Ventura coast is the last southerly bastion where Highway 101 winds close to the water with readily available beach access before reaching the limits of Los Angeles County.

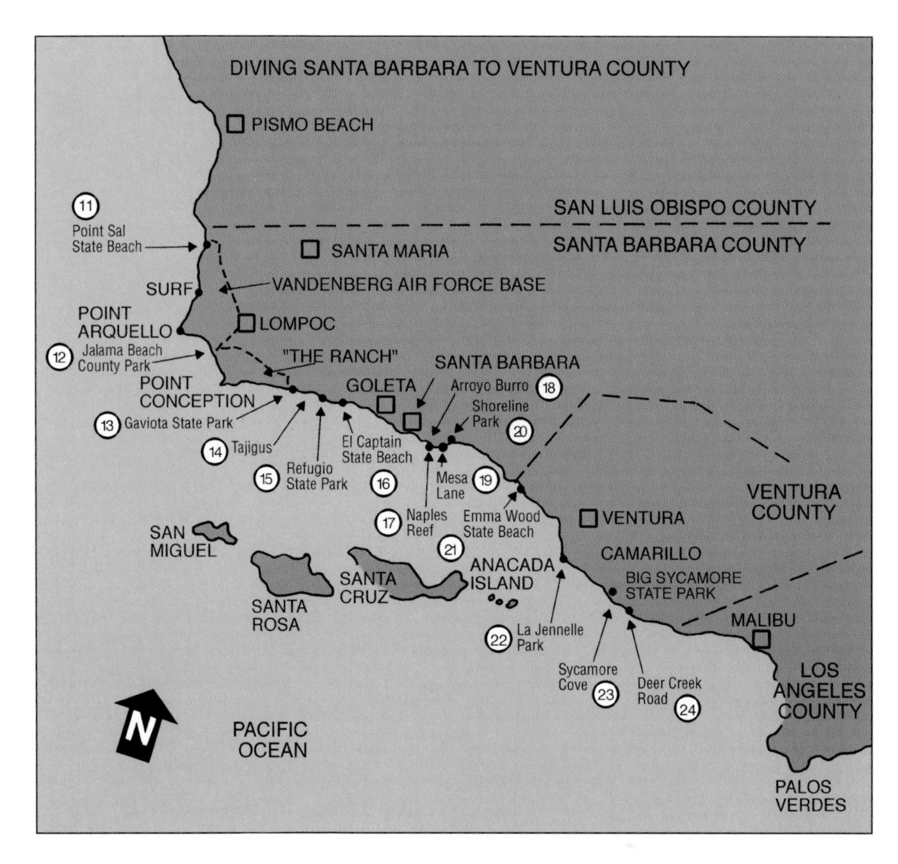

Maturing sheepshead, such as this one, undergo a color transformation from dusty rose to the distinct red and darker tones of the adult male.

Emma Wood State Beach 21

Typical depth range:	Shallow: 10–20 feet
Access:	Park gate located off Old Pacific Coast Highway 1 at Highway 101 junction
Water entry:	Small rocks and boulders
Snorkeling:	Usually poor
Rating:	Intermediate
Visibility:	5–15 feet

How would you like to pull the old motor home or van right up to the edge of the water and set up camp? This 100-acre campsite extends as far south as the Ventura River, but the best diving is found in the northern section by the sea wall. Here, divers can carry their gear a short distance from base camp, lower it down from the seawall, and prepare to visit Emma Wood's offshore reefs. The beach is mostly cobblestone with only a little sand, making entering and exiting the water a bit tricky on the slippery rocks. Nicknamed "Cobblestones" by local surfers, the southern end of the park breaks moderately during any winter swell, which can add to low visibility conditions. During summer months, divers can stick to the northern section of beach and will encounter offshore reefs nearly half a mile from shore.

Even though visibility can be marginal at times, Emma Wood features kelp beds, rocky reefs and sandy areas that are good hunting grounds for halibut. Photography isn't the greatest here except for unusual days of exceptional water clarity (summer is often best due to lack of swell). Divers have been known to bag a lobster or two beneath Emma Wood's offshore ledges. Anemones and nudibranchs are common, as are a variety of sea stars.

The best feature at Emma Wood is the facilities. Camping is permitted, and this is a popular spot among the recreational vehicle set. After all, who wouldn't mind waking up to a warm cup of coffee on a brisk morning only a few yards from the beach and then go diving?

Emma Wood State Beach in Ventura provides camping, diving, fishing, and surfing near the coastal pines with easy water access.

The Spanish shawl nudibranch is one of the most colorful and prolific varieties of nudibranch found along the California coast.

La Jennelle Park 22

Typical depth range:	10–50 feet, deeper near submarine canyon
Access:	South end of Island View Dr. near the jetty
Water entry:	Breakwater rocky entry
Snorkeling:	Good
Rating:	Novice–intermediate
Visibility:	10–35 feet

This one is a little tricky to find because it is situated against the U.S. Navy SEABEE (Construction Battalion) complex to the south.

La Jennelle Park at Port Hueneme is Ventura County's best dive spot, if not one of the best along the Southern California coast. Ironically, few outsiders know of this site. It shouldn't be long before divers of all skill levels discover this marvelous area, where Hueneme submarine canyon comes to the edge of park, creating good diving conditions and some interesting wreck diving.

The park is named for the 467-foot luxury liner that ran aground on April 13, 1970. Instead of being salvaged, the vessel was surrounded with rock and concrete. As a result, very little of the ship remains exposed. But the peninsula it created at the mouth of Port Hueneme shelters a protected swimming area, which is now home to a variety of fish.

To reach the park, exit Highway 1 in Oxnard to Channel Islands Boulevard. Proceed west through Oxnard to the town of Port Hueneme. Turn left on Victoria. The road runs adjacent to Channel Islands Harbor and changes

La Jennelle Beach is situated next to the U.S. Navy Construction Battalion (Sea Bees) base at Port Hueneme. Waters beyond the fence are restricted, although some divers access the south side of the breakwater.

The wall mural, "The La Jennelle" depicts the date and sinking of the former passenger freighter along Silver Strand Beach.

to Roosevelt as it swings to the left. Follow Roosevelt until it becomes Island View Avenue. This dead-ends into Sawtelle Avenue, where you turn right. At the end of Sawtelle Avenue is a gate on a small road that leads to the beach. Proceed through the gate to the small parking lot. La Jennelle Park and the diving area are to the south.

One of the best features of this dive site is the easy water entry. Follow the block wall and fence that face the beach. This will bring you to a large hole in a tattered chain link fence. Enter from a point just a few feet down the rocks, adjacent to the breakwater. The water here is usually tranquil, except when southerly swells reach inside the harbor. You can also enter the water from the rocks at various locations.

In front of the short pier is a small reef covered with kelp. This is a good area for snorkeling and check-out dives when the water is clear. Along the jetty, the bottom drops gradually to 40 feet. Beyond the edge of the jetty, the bottom drops quickly into the submarine canyon.

Kelp beds cover the rocks in the shallow waters, providing a refuge for Garibaldi and other varieties of fish. The best selection of fish can be found in deeper water near the end of the breakwater. Red and orange gorgonians add a splash of color, as do starfish, anemones, sea urchins, and other invertebrates. Sheep crabs are also common.

Occasionally you'll see a lobster near the rocks and the submarine canyon has been known to attract some large fish. If you venture into the canyon, do be careful. The bottom drops off quickly and you'll need to stay clear of the harbor mouth. Loose boulders can be found on the canyon slope at 70–80 feet.

Around the tip of the jetty the water becomes shallow near the rocks, and heavy surge makes diving difficult. But the shallow area inside the park, across from the beach, offers excellent snorkeling conditions.

Sycamore Cove 23

Typical depth range:	25–60 feet
Access:	Park entrance south of Point Mugu, across Highway 1 from campgrounds
Water entry:	Sandy beach
Snorkeling:	Poor
Rating:	Intermediate–advanced
Visibility:	15–35 feet. Sometimes better.

In the early 1960s Sycamore Cove was a private trailer park on leased state land. The State of California evicted all residents by 1972 and prepared a public beach with fire pits, restrooms, picnic tables, and parking. A private fishing pier was demolished during the transition; however, a former recreation room serves as lifeguard headquarters for the area—and for good reason. The north end of the cove features a cement seawall and rocky headland with good diving and some of the strongest currents in the area. In the winter, Sycamore can break with a sizable swell; hence, the surfer's nickname, "Super Tubes."

When calm however, the sand adjacent to the rocks slopes deeply towards 60 feet. The rest of the underwater terrain is sand, except for the southern end of the cove, which has a smaller rocky promontory. Sand dollar beds, as well as California halibut and sole, are found between the rocks. Migrating gray whales are known to frequent the area to scrape barnacles off their skin on the sandy bottom. Dolphin and porpoise are encountered here as well.

This porcelain white droid feeds on a stone coral polyp atop a rocky reef.

A diver inspects sand dollars found at Big Sycamore State Park slightly north of the Los Angeles county line.

Avoid diving the rocky areas during periods of current and swell. The area can become dicey at best. When calm prevails, divers may explore the invertebrate found along the extension of rocky headlands. Sycamore Stream runs for miles into the adjacent canyon and forms a lagoon beneath the bridge at Highway 1. Camping and hiking on the other side of Pacific Coast Highway are excellent.

Deer Creek Road 24

Typical depth range:	15–35 feet
Access:	Stairs at junction of Deer Creek Road and Highway 1
Water entry:	Sandy beach, few rocks
Snorkeling:	Fair
Rating:	Novice–intermediate
Visibility:	10–30 feet

At the farthest point south along the coastline of Ventura County, near Point Mugu, the shore becomes rugged and rocky. At some points, Highway 1 comes very close to the water's edge, but access is still limited. Enter the beach from a short stairway where Pacific Coast Highway intersects with Deer Creek Road. From the top of the stairs you can see a series of kelp beds 50–300 yards offshore. The stairway leads to a sandy beach where surf entry is possible. Reefs free of kelp are situated about 50 feet out in 15 feet of water.

A thick kelp bed stretches out 200 yards from shore to a depth of 35 feet. The rich kelp hunting ground harbors bass, sheepshead, and opaleye. Nudibranchs, sponge, urchins, starfish, lobster, abalone, and scallops can be found

Deer Creek Road is a rocky dive area with large kelp patches within 200 yards of shore. The access to the beach, however, can be limited.

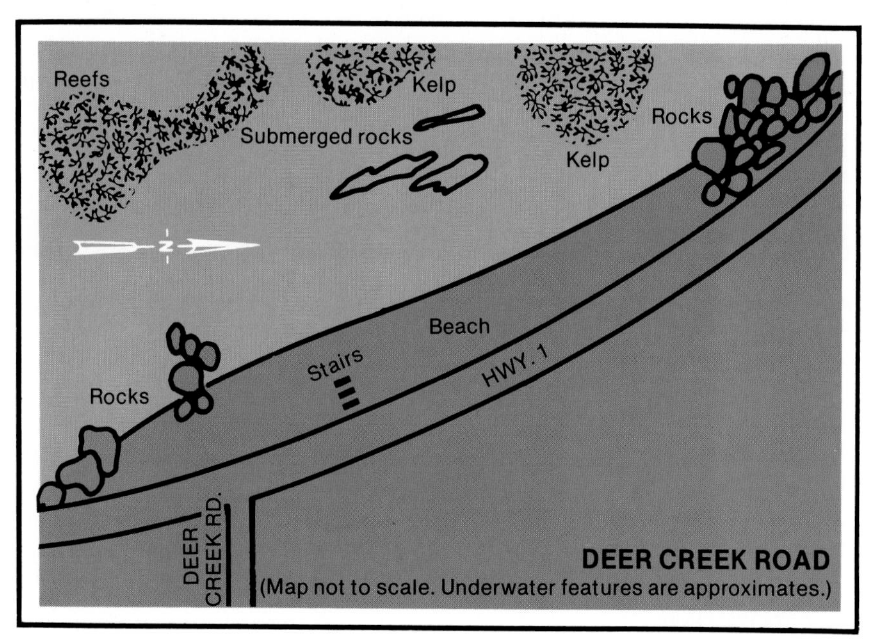

Large sea stars and other colorful invertebrates are found throughout the shallow reefs.

Here a sand star visits a sand dollar bed.

on the rocks. Check the sand adjacent to the reefs for large halibut and rays. The lucky diver may also encounter dolphins, seals, or a gray whale on the seaward side of the reef.

Although the reefs come in fairly close to shore, the better diving is only a short swim away. The spot is open to heavy surf, so be prepared for changes in surge and visibility. With a two- to three-foot swell, visibility beneath the kelp averages 10 feet; outside the reef, visibility reaches 20–30 feet. High surf that creates a bottom surge can reduce visibility significantly.

6

Safety

Diving the southern Monterey–Ventura County areas along California's coast can be a safe and enjoyable experience. Be sure to evaluate conditions before going in the water and heed the cautions listed in each individual dive site. It is important to remember that nothing is 100 percent safe, and divers must be responsible for making the right decisions to avoid error. There are, however, a few safety points that should be elaborated upon to help.

Proper Weighting. Unfortunately many divers venture seaward with more lead on their belts than they really need. This causes stress and discomfort. Be sure you are using the proper amount of weight that is right for you, and remember, just because you learned to dive with a certain amount of weight doesn't mean you can use less as you become a more relaxed and proficient diver.

Buoyancy Control. This relates to proper weighting to a degree. If divers cannot control their ascents and descents, they may find themselves stuck on the bottom or ascending too quickly. Swim to the surface slowly, vent air from your BC, and don't use the power inflater on ascent. When you are venturing to deeper depths, be sure to inflate your vest to maintain neutral buoyancy.

Hypothermia. Occasionally divers get too cold. When the body gets numb, so does the brain. If you find yourself shivering uncontrollably, get out of the water and get warm. The northern end of the Central California coast is especially known for its colder waters.

Surf and rocky entries. These usually appear to be trickier than they actually are. Still, no one wants to crash onto a rock or get pounded in the surf zone. Gauge your entries and exits carefully. Timing is important when water is rising or falling quickly.

Hazardous marine animals. Most marine critters are docile. You can hurt yourself by coming in contact with sea urchins. They are not attack-trained, but if you crash into one, it can be painful. Although rare in this area, moray eels are docile until harassed. Don't stick your hand in a crevice; they

This thick-horn aleoid is another colorful nudibranch found in Golden State waters from Big Sur to Ventura.

may bite. Sting rays can deliver a powerful barbed lash if stepped on. These animals inhabit the sandy plains, so it's a good idea to shuffle your fins during entry to let them know you are coming so they can get out of the way. Rockfish and scorpion fish have spines that can deliver a venomous sting if you place your hand on one.

Steer clear of the bold and aggressive Pacific electric ray (a.k.a. Torpedo Ray). These cousins to sharks often swim right up to the divers. Don't pet one because they pack a significant wallop. Their frontal lobes can deliver quite an electric shock.

Scuba Diving Related Emergencies

On Shore: If a hyperbaric accident is suspected upon returning to the beach, contact the paramedics. There is a recompression chamber in the Monterey Bay area. In Ventura/Santa Barbara areas contact Los Robles Medical Center (805) 497-2727. If you are unsure who to contact in the event of a diving emergency, contact DAN (the Divers Alert Network).

Something to Remember: Avoid dealing with emergency rooms and hospitals unless specifically referred to by knowledgeable medical personnel. Most physicians are not familiar with decompression sickness and hyperbaric injuries. Deal directly with recompression facilities. If in doubt, contact DAN. They will put you in touch with a hyperbaric physician and proper treatment facility.

Diving Accidents in south Monterey to Los Angeles counties. Using the California-wide 911 number is not the best option in a diving accident where decompression sickness or an air embolism may be suspected. However, it is okay for trauma and "slip and fall" problems.

U.S. Coast Guard Emergency Coordination Center
(310) 590-2225

Divers Alert Network (DAN)
(919) 684-2948

Be certain to inform your point of contact that this is a diving-related accident. Give your location and stand by for further instructions.

Garibaldi are not as common along the Central California coast as they are farther south, although divers still encounter them. Here, a Garibaldi swims across a reef with a calico bass.

Spanish shawl nudibranch are frequently found in the waters off the Central California coast.

And Finally. Know your personal diving skill limitations! Don't jump into the ocean on a day you don't feel up to it, or are really out of your league. Remember, diving the Central California coast is a little wild. If you are new to diving these areas and are unsure of your abilities in this different environment, contact a local instructor or a divemaster for an orientation to the area.

Additionally, always plan and execute your dive within preset, pre-dive parameters. Discuss depth, time, and air supply limits with your diving partner.

Weather Information

The climatic conditions from the Big Sur coastline to Ventura County can cover a wide range. The northern spectrum of the central coast is more prone to the effects of wind, swell, and storm than its southern neighbor; but, that does not mean the diving is less hospitable on a whole. The diversity of prevailing weather and sea conditions still should not be taken lightly.

One of the best methods to determine how weather will affect a dive site you visit is by watching local television news. The detailed satellite maps many stations show are invaluable for predicting approaching offshore weather fronts. On the other hand, television surf reports are not always accurate. Get a confirmation on each report by calling any of the following phone numbers:

Offshore weather from Monterey to the Mexican border
(310) 477-1463

Ventura County
(805) 644-8338

Santa Barbara County
(805) 962-SURF

Local surf reports are often recorded by beach lifeguards (or park rangers in the northern areas). Often, these are updated throughout the day.

Rugged and raw, the Big Sur Coast beckons divers.

Appendix

The list below is included as a service to the reader. The list is as accurate as possible at the time of printing. This list does not constitute an endorsement of these facilities. If operators/owners wish to be included in future reprints/editions, please contact Pisces Books, P.O. Box 2608, Houston, Texas 77252-2608

Dive Operators

Innerspace Divers
N. Chester Ave.
Bakersfield
(805) 399-1425

Captain Frog's Scuba
2500 New Stine #307
Bakersfield
(805) 833-3781

Aquarius Dive Shop
2240 Del Monte Ave.
Monterey
(408) 375-1933

The Scuba Outlet
9500 Rosedale Hwy.
Bakersfield
(805) 589-3648

Aquarius Dive Shop
32 Cannery Row, #4
Monterey
(408) 375-6605

Bamboo Reef
614 Lighthouse Ave.
Monterey
(408) 372-1685

The Dive Shop of Santa Maria
1975 South Broadway
Santa Maria
(805) 922-0076

Dive West Sports
115 W. Main
Santa Maria
(805) 925-5878

Watersports Unlimited
732 N. H St.
Lompoc
(805) 736-1800

Diving Locker
500 Botello Rd.
Goleta
(805) 967-4456

Divers Supply of Santa Barbara
5822 Hollister Ave.
Goleta (805) 964-0180

Aquatics of Santa Barbara
5370 Hollister #3
Santa Barbara
(805) 964-8689

Anacapa Aquatics
22 Anacapa St.
Santa Barbara
(805) 963-8917

Underwater Sports
Breakwater Harbor
Santa Barbara
(805) 962-5400

Aqua Adventures
2172 Pickwick Dr.
Camarillo
(805) 647-8344

Ventura Dive & Sport
1559 Spinnaker #108
Ventura
(805) 650-6500

Channel Islands Scuba
1495 Palma #C
Ventura
(805) 644-DIVE

Aquatics
695 Channel Islands Blvd.
Port Hueneme
(805) 984-DIVE

Sport Chalet Divers
1885 Ventura Blvd.
Oxnard
(805) 485-5222

American Diving
1901 Pacific Coast Hwy.
Lomita
(213) 326-6663

Dive N' Surf
504 W. Broadway
Redondo Beach
(213) 372-8423

Blue Cheer
1110 Wilshire Blvd.
Santa Monica
(213) 828-1217

Malibu Divers
21231 Pacific Coast Hwy.
Malibu
(213) 456-2396

Scuba Haus
2501 Wilshire Blvd.
Santa Monica
(213) 828-2916

Reef Seekers Dive Co.
8542 Wilshire Blvd.
Beverly Hills

Sea D' Sea
1911 Catalina Ave.
Redondo Beach
(213) 373-6355

Marina Dive & Sport
141 West 22nd St.
San Pedro
(213) 831-5647

Sport Chalet Divers
920 Foothill Blvd.
La Canada
(818) 790-9800

Sport Chalet Divers
24200 W. Lyons Ave.
Valencia
(805) 253-3883

Scuba Duba Dive
7126 Reseda Blvd.
Reseda
(818) 881-4545

Desert Scuba
44441 N. Sierra Hwy.
Lancaster
(805) 948-8883

Divers Corner
12045 Paramount Blvd.
Downey
(213) 869-7702

New England Divers
4148 Viking Way
Long Beach
(213) 421-8939 or (714) 827-5110

Gucciones Scuba Habitat
2843 #A Diamond Bar Blvd.
Diamond Bar
(714) 594-7927

Diver's West
2333 E. Foothill Blvd.
Pasadena
(818) 796-4287

Sport Diving West
11501 Whittier Blvd.
Whittier
(213) 692-7373

Pacific Wilderness & Ocean Sports
1719 S. Pacific Ave.
San Pedro
(213) 833-2422

Aquatic Image Expeditions
2355 Foothill Blvd. #261
La Verne
(818) 852-2028

Sarcas Ski & Sport
2451 #B Foothill Blvd.
La Verne
(714) 596-4946

Antelope Valley Scuba
1430 W. Ave. I
Antelope Valley
(805) 949-2555

A diver cruises through a kelp bed off Santa Barbara's beaches.

Index

Be sure to check out these other great books from Pisces:

Great Reefs of the World
Watching Fishes: Understanding Coral Reef Fish Behavior
Skin Diver Magazine's Book of Fishes, 2nd Edition
Shooting Underwater Video: A Complete Guide to the Equipment and Techniques for Shooting, Editing, and Post-Production
Guide to Shipwreck Diving: New York & New Jersey
Guide to Shipwreck Diving: North Carolina
Guide to Shipwreck Diving: Southern California

Diving and Snorkeling Guides to:

Australia: Coral Sea and Great Barrier Reef
Australia: Southeast Coast and Tasmania
The Bahamas: Family Islands and Grand Bahama
The Bahamas: Nassau and New Providence Island 2nd Edition
Belize
Bonaire
The British Virgin Islands
The Cayman Islands 2nd Edition
The Channel Islands
Cozumel, 2nd Edition
Curaçao
Fiji
Florida's East Coast, 2nd Edition
The Florida Keys, 2nd Edition
The Great Lakes
The Hawaiian Islands, 2nd Edition
Northern California and the Monterey Peninsula, 2nd Edition
The Pacific Northwest
Roatan and Honduras' Bay Islands
Texas
The Turks and Caicos Islands
The U.S. Virgin Islands, 2nd Edition

Available from your favorite dive shop, bookstore, or directly from the publisher: Pisces Books™, a division of Gulf Publishing Company, Book Division, Dept. AD, P.O. Box 2608, Houston, Texas 77252-2608 (713) 520-4444.